« MINECRAFT »
MINING

UNOFFICIAL GAMER GUIDE

Zelda Wagner

Lerner Publications ◆ Minneapolis

Lerner Publications Company
An imprint of Lerner Publishing Group, Inc.
241 First Avenue North
Minneapolis, MN 55401 USA

For reading levels and more information, look up this title at www.lernerbooks.com.

Main body text set in ITC Franklin Gothic Std.
Typeface provided by Adobe Systems.

Editor: Angel Kidd **Designer:** Mary Ross **Photo Editor:** Angel Kidd
Lerner team: Martha Kranes

Library of Congress Cataloging-in-Publication Data

Names: Wagner, Zelda, 2000– author.
Title: Minecraft mining : unofficial gamer guide / Zelda Wagner.
Description: Minneapolis, MN : Lerner Publications, [2025] | Series: UpDog books. Minecraft zone | Includes bibliographical references and index. | Audience: Ages 8–11 | Audience: Grades 2–3 | Summary: "There are many adventures, dangers, and rewards to be found while mining in Minecraft. Readers will love exploring the caves of Minecraft and learning about the tools they need to gather ores and materials"— Provided by publisher.
Identifiers: LCCN 2023034463 (print) | LCCN 2023034464 (ebook) | ISBN 9798765626528 (library binding) | ISBN 9798765629062 (paperback) | ISBN 9798765635568 (epub)
Subjects: LCSH: Minecraft (Game)—Juvenile literature. | Mines and mineral resources—Juvenile literature.
Classification: LCC GV1469.35.M535 W3426 2025 (print) | LCC GV1469.35. M535 (ebook) | DDC 794.8/5—dc23/eng/20230721

LC record available at https://lccn.loc.gov/2023034463
LC ebook record available at https://lccn.loc.gov/2023034464

Manufactured in the United States of America
1-1010173-51986-11/27/2023

TaBLe OF CONTeNTS

Mining is a big part of playing *Minecraft* in Survival Mode.

To start mining, players craft a wooden pickaxe.

Players can mine in caves.
Or they can dig their own
tunnels underground.

Players mine to find ores. Copper and iron are common ores.

Coal smelts ores
into ingots.

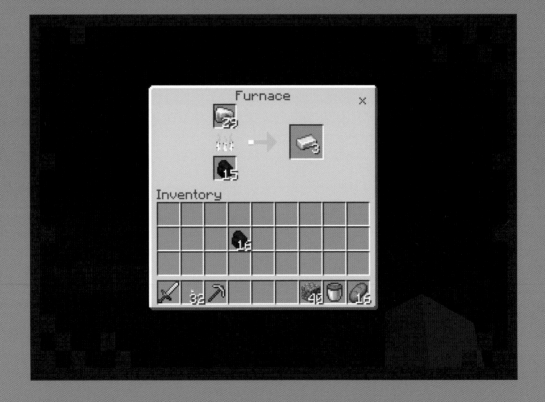

Some ingots are used
to craft tools and armor.

« UP NEXT! »

WATCH OUT!

MANY DANGERS

Players should avoid digging straight up or down. They can get buried or fall to their deaths!

Making a staircase
is safer.

Hostile mobs might attack
players while mining. Weapons
are used to fight them.

Wearing armor makes
fighting mobs easier.

A shield can block arrows
and explosions.

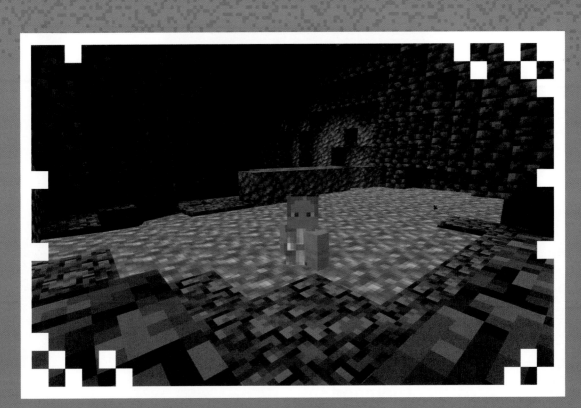

Players can run into lava in
mines. Be careful not to fall in!

GAME BREAK!

Here are the five rarest ores in *Minecraft*:

1. **Ancient debris**

2. **Emerald**

3. **Diamond**

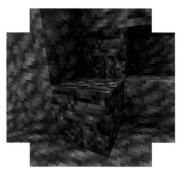

4. **Lapis lazuli**

5. **Gold**

These are the most important things for mining:

1.   Pickaxe

2.   Weapon

3.   Torches

4.   Food

5.   Shovel

《 **UP NEXT!** 》

UPGRADES.

STRONGER TOOLS

Some ores are rare. It can be hard to find them.

Players search for rare ores such
as diamonds deep underground.

Players use a diamond pickaxe to mine ancient debris in the Nether.

Ancient debris helps craft netherite. It makes the strongest tools in *Minecraft*.

Players use a smithing table to upgrade diamond gear to netherite.

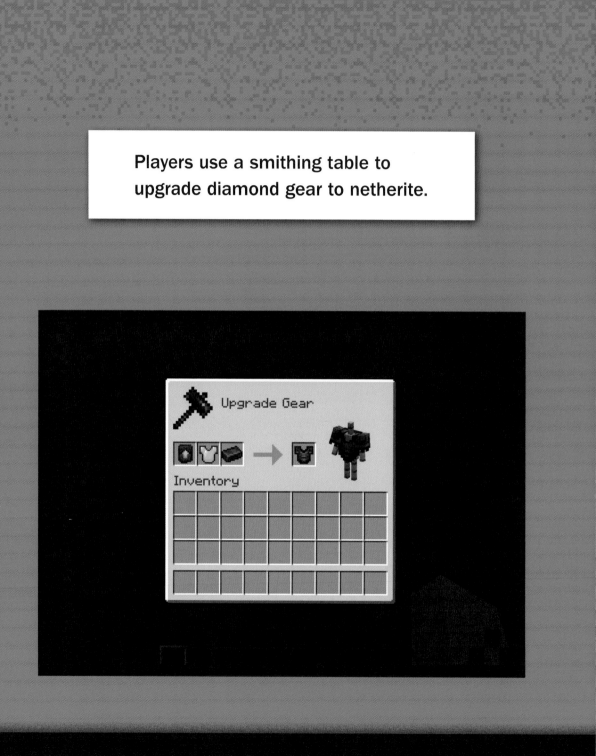

Fortune is a helpful enchantment. It gives players more materials from mining.

UP NEXT! >>

LOOK AT THAT!

COOL CAVES

Lots of mobs roam
in big caves.

Glow berries grow in
the lush cave biome.

Dripstone spikes can grow
from cave floors or ceilings.

Mineshafts and monster rooms can be found in caves.

Wardens guard ancient
cities in the deep dark.

Every mining trip is an adventure. Now you're ready to explore the caves!

Glossary

biome: a large region and the plants and animals that live there

craft: to make something out of materials

hostile mob: a creature that attacks players

smelt: to melt an ore into a useable metal ingot

upgrade: to make something better

Check It Out!

Britannica Kids: *Minecraft*
https://kids.britannica.com/students/article/
Minecraft/631450

Kiddle: *Minecraft* Facts for Kids
https://kids.kiddle.co/Minecraft

McBrien, Thomas. Minecraft: *Guide to Survival*. New York:
Del Rey, 2022.

Miller, Marie-Therese. *34 Amazing Facts about* Minecraft.
Minneapolis: Lerner Publications, 2024.

Minecraft Official Site
https://www.minecraft.net/en-us

Wagner, Zelda. Minecraft *Farming*. Minneapolis: Lerner
Publications, 2025.

Index

Photo Acknowledgments

Image credits: Various screenshots by Angel Kidd. Design elements: Anatolii Poliashenko/Getty Images; filo/Getty Images.